# QUICKREADS

*LEVEL E • BOOK 1*

Elfrieda H. Hiebert, Ph.D.

Glenview, Illinois

Boston, Massachusetts

Chandler, Arizona

Upper Saddle River, New Jersey

ALWAYS LEARNING

PEARSON

**Program Reviewers and Consultants**

**Dr. Barbara A. Baird**
Director of Federal Programs/Richardson ISD
Richardson, TX

**Dr. Kate Kinsella**
Dept. of Secondary Education and Step to College Program
San Francisco State University
San Francisco, CA

**Pat Sears**
Early Childhood Coordinator/Virginia Beach Public Schools
Virginia Beach, VA

**Dr. Judith B. Smith**
Supervisor of ESOL and World and Classical Languages/Baltimore City Public Schools
Baltimore, MD

Acknowledgments appear on page 9, which constitutes an extension of this copyright page.

ISBN-13: 978-1-4284-3158-4
ISBN-10:   1-4284-3158-6
1 2 3 4 5 6 7 8 9 10 V011 15 14 13 12 11

# CONTENTS

SCIENCE ## Marine Animals Without Backbones

Marine Invertebrates . . . . . . . . . . . . . . . . . . . . . 10

Stingers . . . . . . . . . . . . . . . . . . . . . . . . . . . . 12

Mollusks . . . . . . . . . . . . . . . . . . . . . . . . . . . . 14

Outer Skeletons . . . . . . . . . . . . . . . . . . . . . . . 16

Sea Stars . . . . . . . . . . . . . . . . . . . . . . . . . . . 18

**Marine Animals Without Backbones
Review** . . . . . . . . . . . . . . . . . . . . . . . . . . . . 20

 Connect Your Ideas . . . . . . . . . . . . . . . . . . . 23

# CONTENTS

SCIENCE **Plants and People**

Plants and Life on Earth . . . . . . . . . . . . . . . . . . . . . 24

The Biggest and the Best . . . . . . . . . . . . . . . . . . . 26

Pluots and Apriums . . . . . . . . . . . . . . . . . . . . . . . 28

Special Ways to Grow Plants . . . . . . . . . . . . . . . . 30

What's Next for People and Plants? . . . . . . . . . . . 32

**Plants and People Review** . . . . . . . . . . . . . . . . . 34

Connect Your Ideas . . . . . . . . . . . . . . . . . . . . 37

SCIENCE  **Food and Nutrition**

Eating Right . . . . . . . . . . . . . . . . . . . . . . . 38

The Food Pyramid . . . . . . . . . . . . . . . . . . . 40

Nutrition Labels . . . . . . . . . . . . . . . . . . . . . 42

Water Supply . . . . . . . . . . . . . . . . . . . . . . . 44

Bugs for Dinner? . . . . . . . . . . . . . . . . . . . . 46

**Food and Nutrition Review** . . . . . . . . . . . . 48

Connect Your Ideas . . . . . . . . . . . . . . . . . 51

# CONTENTS

SOCIAL STUDIES

## Civil Rights Leaders

Civil Rights . . . . . . . . . . . . . . . . . . . . . . 52

Equal Rights . . . . . . . . . . . . . . . . . . . . . . 54

Equal Education . . . . . . . . . . . . . . . . . . . 56

Equal Treatment . . . . . . . . . . . . . . . . . . 58

Children's Rights . . . . . . . . . . . . . . . . . . 60

**Civil Rights Leaders Review** . . . . . . . . . . . . . . 62

 Connect Your Ideas. . . . . . . . . . . . . . . . . . 65

SOCIAL
STUDIES

# The 50 American States

American States . . . . . . . . . . . . . . . . . . . . . . . . 66

State Governments . . . . . . . . . . . . . . . . . . . . . 68

Learning and Playing in States . . . . . . . . . . . . . . . 70

State Symbols . . . . . . . . . . . . . . . . . . . . . . . . 72

Local Governments . . . . . . . . . . . . . . . . . . . . . 74

**The 50 American States Review** . . . . . . . . . . . 76

 Connect Your Ideas . . . . . . . . . . . . . . . . . . . 79

# CONTENTS

SOCIAL STUDIES

## The United States and the World Community

The World Community. . . . . . . . . . . . . . . . . . . . . . . 80

The United Nations . . . . . . . . . . . . . . . . . . . . . . . 82

The Peace Corps. . . . . . . . . . . . . . . . . . . . . . . . . 84

The Olympic Games . . . . . . . . . . . . . . . . . . . . . . 86

The International Space Station . . . . . . . . . . . . . . . 88

**The United States and the World Community Review**. . . . . . . . . . . . . . . . . . . . . . 90

 Connect Your Ideas. . . . . . . . . . . . . . . . . . . . 93

**Reading Log** . . . . . . . . . . . . . . . . . . . . . . . . 94

**Self-Check Graph** . . . . . . . . . . . . . . . . . . . . 96

# Acknowledgments

## Photographs

Every effort has been made to secure permission and provide appropriate credit for photographic material. The publisher deeply regrets any omission and pledges to correct errors called to its attention in subsequent editions.

Unless otherwise acknowledged, all photographs are the property of Pearson Education, Inc.

Photo locators denoted as follows: Top (T), Center (C), Bottom (B), Left (L), Right (R), Background (Bkgd)

**Cover:** Design Pics/Sean White/Thinkstock; **3** ©DK Images; **4** ©Liseykina/Shutterstock; **5** Thinkstock; **6** ©RW3/NewsCom; **7** ©Marmaduke St. John/Alamy Images; **8** MSFC/NASA; **10** ©David Fleetham/Alamy Images; **12** ©Kavram/Shutterstock; **14** Photos to Go/Photolibrary; **16** ©DK Images; **18** ©Cigdem Sean Cooper/ Shutterstock; **24** ©Liseykina/Shutterstock; **26** ©Aleksko/Shutterstock; **28** Photos to Go/Photolibrary; **30** ©Beat Bieler/Shutterstock; **32** (TR) ©Anne Kitzman/Shutterstock, (BL) ©Grafvision/Shutterstock; **38** Thinkstock; **40** (meat and beans) ©D. Hurst/Alamy, (Vegetables) ©Monkey Business Images/Shutterstock, (milk, grains) ©Morgan Lane Photography/Shutterstock, (fruit) Getty Images, USDA; **44** Stockbyte/ Getty Images; **46** (R) ©dbimages/Alamy Images, (BL) ©Robert Harding Picture Library Ltd./Alamy Images, (TL) ©Stuart Dunn Travel/Alamy Images; **52** ©Hulton Archive/Getty Images; **54** Library of Congress; **56** ©AP Images; **58** Corbis; **60** ©RW3/NewsCom; **66** National Archives; **68** Medioimages/Photodisc/Thinkstock; **70** ©Marmaduke St. John/Alamy Images; **72** (BL) ©Wally Bauman Photography/ Alamy, (TR) Medioimages/Photodisc/Thinkstock, (C) Thomas Northcut/ Thinkstock; **74** ©Jerry Sharp/Shutterstock; **80** ©David R. Frazier Photolibrary, Inc./Alamy; **82** ©JRC, Inc./Alamy Images; **84** ©Ernest Manewal/SuperStock; **86** ©Eileen Langsley Olympic Images/Alamy Images; **88** MSFC/NASA.

# Marine Animals Without Backbones

The ocean allows marine invertebrates to move around easily. The marine invertebrate in this picture is an octopus.

# Marine Invertebrates

The bones that run up the middle of your back provide support and help you move. People and other animals with backbones are [25] called vertebrates. Vertebrates make up five percent of Earth's animals. The other 95 percent do not have backbones. They are called invertebrates. Animals without backbones [50] are like jelly. They need support to hold their bodies together and to move.

The ocean is a perfect home for invertebrates because the water [75] helps them move and trap food. There are many kinds of marine invertebrates, and they differ in how they look, move, and protect themselves. In [100] spite of their differences, all marine invertebrates have two things in common: They live in water, and they don't have backbones. [121]

# Marine Animals Without Backbones

The tentacles of these jellyfish hang down as they swim in the ocean.

# Stingers

Jellyfish are about 95 percent water. They have no heart, brain, bones, or eyes. Most jellyfish have rounded bodies with long, thin tentacles, or [25] feelers, that hang down. Often a favorite at aquariums, jellyfish move by pumping water through their soft bodies. These marine invertebrates seem to dance as [50] they move up and down.

While jellyfish are a favorite at aquariums, they are called "stingers" for good reason. Their tentacles contain poison that stings [75] other animals they touch. Jellyfish use their stinging tentacles to protect themselves and to catch food. One jellyfish, called the sea wasp, poses a special [100] danger to swimmers. If people are badly stung by a sea wasp, they can die in as little as four minutes. [121]

# Marine Animals Without Backbones

Snails are a kind of mollusk with a hard shell.

# Mollusks

A large group of marine invertebrates is classified as mollusks. Clams, snails, and octopuses are examples of mollusks. Mollusks have three main parts: a [25] head, a body, and a foot. The head contains sense organs and a brain. The body contains internal organs. The foot is often used to [50] grasp something solid, like rocks.

Most animals that are classified as mollusks have hard shells. These hard shells protect the mollusk's internal organs. However, some [75] mollusks, like octopuses, do not have hard shells. Octopuses can swim, unlike hard-shelled mollusks, which usually move around slowly on the ocean floor. Octopuses [100] also protect themselves by squirting ink into the water. Their ink makes it difficult to see octopuses as they quickly swim away. [122]

# Marine Animals Without Backbones

Crustaceans, like this crab, have their skeletons on the outside of their bodies.

# Outer Skeletons

Crabs and shrimp belong to a group of marine invertebrates called crustaceans. Crustaceans, like crabs and shrimp, are often called shellfish. However, crustaceans [25] are not fish. They have shells or skeletons, which are on the outside, not on the inside as they are in fish and other vertebrates. [50]

Crabs, shrimp, and other crustaceans have several pairs of legs. Their bodies and legs have joints like those that humans have at their knees and [75] elbows.

Crabs can swim, but some crustaceans, like shrimp, can only move along the ocean floor. Other crustaceans, like barnacles, spend their lives in one [100] place. Barnacles fix themselves to rocks, ships, and even whales. When water pours over them, barnacles reach out their little legs to get food. [124]

# Marine Animals Without Backbones

The spiny skin of this sea star protects it from other animals.

# Sea Stars

Sea stars are often called star fish. However, their proper name is *sea star* because, unlike fish, they have neither backbones nor fins.[25] Sea stars are members of the echinoderm family of marine invertebrates. *Echinoderm* means "spiny skin" in the Greek language. Echinoderms, like sea stars or sea[50] cucumbers, have little spikes or bumps covering their skin.

Sea cucumbers are shaped like the food after which they are named. Like their cousins the[75] sea stars, sea cucumbers have rows of tiny feet on one side of their bodies. These feet are shaped like tubes. When water enters one[100] of these tiny feet, the tube expands. This movement allows sea stars, sea cucumbers, and other echinoderms to crawl along the ocean floor.[123]

Write words that will help you remember what you learned.

### Marine Invertebrates

_____
_____
_____
_____

### Stingers

_____
_____
_____
_____

### Mollusks

_____
_____
_____
_____

### Outer Skeletons

_____
_____
_____
_____

### Sea Stars

_____
_____
_____
_____

## Marine Invertebrates

**1.** An invertebrate is an animal _____

    Ⓐ that lives in the ocean.

    Ⓑ without a backbone.

    Ⓒ with fins.

    Ⓓ with a backbone.

**2.** How are invertebrates different from vertebrates?

_____

_____

_____

## Stingers

**1.** "Stingers" is MAINLY about _____

    Ⓐ the stingers of jellyfish.

    Ⓑ sea wasps.

    Ⓒ jellyfish.

    Ⓓ how jellyfish dance.

**2.** Describe how jellyfish look and move.

_____

_____

_____

## Mollusks

**1.** The three main parts of mollusks are _____

    Ⓐ the head, the body, and the foot.

    Ⓑ the sense organs, the brain, and the head.

    Ⓒ the shell, the sense organs, and ink.

    Ⓓ the shell, the head, and the body.

**2.** Describe how two different kinds of mollusks move.

_____

_____

_____

## Outer Skeletons

**1.** Another good name for "Outer Skeletons" is _____

    Ⓐ "Shrimp and Barnacles."

    Ⓑ "Mollusks We Eat."

    Ⓒ "Marine Vertebrates."

    Ⓓ "Crustaceans."

**2.** Name two ways in which crustaceans are different from fish.

_____

_____

_____

## Sea Stars

1. How are sea stars different from fish?

    (A) Sea stars do not have backbones or fins.

    (B) Sea stars have backbones and spiny skin.

    (C) Sea stars are long and have smooth shells.

    (D) Sea stars are marine vertebrates.

2. How do sea stars and sea cucumbers move?

_____

_____

_____

## Connect Your Ideas

1. How are all marine invertebrates alike?

_____

_____

_____

2. Describe how two kinds of marine invertebrates are different.

_____

_____

_____

# Plants and People

The process of photosynthesis lets plants breathe and make food. It also helps people breathe and have food to eat.

# Plants and Life on Earth

Most of the 350,000 kinds of plants that grow on Earth could live without people. However, people could not live[25] without plants. Every kind of food eaten by people comes directly or indirectly from plants. Unlike animals, plants make their own food. Through a process[50] called photosynthesis, plants use sunlight, carbon dioxide, water, and minerals to make their own food.

In photosynthesis, the green leaves of plants soak up sunlight.[75] Leaves also take in a gas called carbon dioxide. The roots of plants gather water and minerals from the soil. During photosynthesis, plants take in[100] carbon dioxide and give off oxygen. People do just the opposite. They breathe in oxygen given off by plants and breathe out carbon dioxide.[124]

# Plants and People

Choosing seeds from the biggest plants has helped farmers grow larger watermelons.

# The Biggest and the Best

In early times, people ate fruits and vegetables that grew in nature. When the plants in one place had been [25] eaten, people traveled until they found more plants. The discovery that fruits and vegetables could be grown by planting seeds led to the first farms. [50] By planting and taking care of crops on farms, people could stay in one place.

Farmers soon discovered that they got better crops by keeping [75] seeds from the best plants and planting them the next year. Farmers also learned that fruit from one tree could grow on other kinds of [100] trees. When a branch from a lemon tree is grafted onto an orange tree, the orange tree produces both oranges and lemons. [122]

# Plants and People

Cross-fertilization has given shoppers a large variety of fruits and vegetables.

# Pluots and Apriums

Farmers have learned to use cross-fertilization to improve plants. In cross-fertilization, the pollen from one plant is used to fertilize[25] the seed of another plant. The seeds that come from cross-fertilization grow new plants with the best parts of the original plants. Cross-fertilization[50] has produced new kinds of wheat that grow well in cold weather.

Cross-fertilization can even produce new fruits and vegetables. Two new fruits are[75] pluots and apriums. Pluots and apriums have been created by cross-fertilizing plums and apricots. Pluots have smooth skins like plums, but taste sweet like[100] apricots. Apriums have fuzzy skins like apricots, but they are dark inside like plums. Apriums taste like a blend of apricots and plums.[123]

# Plants and People

Greenhouses let people grow plants when it is cold outdoors.

# Special Ways to Grow Plants

People want to eat fresh fruits and vegetables, like melons and tomatoes, all year. In many places, however, plants cannot[25] grow outdoors all year. Growing fruit and vegetables in greenhouses has solved this problem.

Greenhouses allow farmers to create warm environments indoors when the environment[50] outdoors is cold. In greenhouses, lights can be turned on at night, making photosynthesis happen faster. By using greenhouses, people can have fresh fruits and[75] vegetables all year.

Some areas have other growing problems. In places where the soil is not rich, plants can be grown in water to which[100] minerals have been added. The process of growing plants in water is called hydroponics. Tomatoes and melons are especially easy to grow with hydroponics.[124]

# Plants and People

The leaves of the willow tree are used to make aspirin.

# What's Next for People and Plants?

Because of the great variety of plants on Earth, many scientists look for new uses for plants. One plant[25] with many uses is corn. For example, raw corn can be processed to make a clean-burning fuel called ethanol. Ethanol can be burned in[50] cars and trucks, either with gasoline or instead of it. Unlike gasoline, the supply of ethanol is not limited. In addition, ethanol does less harm[75] to the environment than gasoline.

Plants are also used to make many medicines. For thousands of years, people have used aspirin for pain. Aspirin comes[100] from the leaves of willow trees. As scientists continue to study plants, discoveries are likely to lead to many new medicines and other products.[124]

Write words that will help you remember what you learned.

## Plants and Life on Earth

_____

_____

_____

_____

## The Biggest and the Best

_____

_____

_____

_____

## Pluots and Apriums

_____

_____

_____

_____

## Special Ways to Grow Plants

_____

_____

_____

_____

## What's Next for People and Plants?

_____

_____

_____

_____

## Plants and Life on Earth

1.  What happens during photosynthesis?

    Ⓐ Plants breathe in oxygen.

    Ⓑ Plants make carbon dioxide.

    Ⓒ Plants give off water.

    Ⓓ Plants make their own food.

2.  How do plants and people help each other breathe?

    _____

    _____

    _____


## The Biggest and the Best

1.  The main idea of "The Biggest and the Best" is that _____

    Ⓐ early people had to travel to find fruits and vegetables.

    Ⓑ over time, people have discovered new ways to grow crops.

    Ⓒ farmers learned to grow many kinds of oranges and lemons.

    Ⓓ fruit from one kind of tree can grow on another kind of tree.

2.  How has farming changed since early times?

    _____

    _____

    _____

# Review Plants and People

## Pluots and Apriums

**1.** What happens during cross-fertilization?

   Ⓐ The seeds from one plant are used to make pluots and apriums.

   Ⓑ Farmers take the seeds from two plants and mix them.

   Ⓒ The pollen from one plant fertilizes the seed from another plant.

   Ⓓ Farmers make apricots and plums.

**2.** What are pluots and apriums?

_____

_____

_____

## Special Ways to Grow Plants

**1.** "Special Ways to Grow Plants" is MAINLY about _____

   Ⓐ growing plants in greenhouses and without soil.

   Ⓑ fruits and vegetables that grow all year.

   Ⓒ how to create different kinds of soil for growing plants.

   Ⓓ ways to grow plants in cold places.

**2.** What is hydroponics?

_____

_____

_____

## What's Next for People and Plants?

1. What are two ways people use plants?

   Ⓐ to make gasoline and willow trees

   Ⓑ to make aspirin and photosynthesis

   Ⓒ to make fuel and medicine

   Ⓓ to make hydroponics and minerals

2. Retell what you learned about one use for plants described in this passage.

   _____

   _____

   _____

## Connect Your Ideas

1. Describe three ways plants are useful to people.

   _____

   _____

   _____

2. Suppose there was another passage in this unit. Do you think it might be about medicines from Earth or how animals help people? Why?

   _____

   _____

   _____

# Food and Nutrition

The nutrients in foods help people stay healthy and give them energy to work and have fun.

# Eating Right

Food gives people health and energy. All foods have nutrients, which are the parts of food that keep people healthy. The five kinds[25] of nutrients are carbohydrates, fats, protein, vitamins, and minerals.

Carbohydrates give people energy. Simple carbohydrates, such as those in sugar, give short bursts of energy.[50] In contrast, complex carbohydrates, such as those in whole-wheat bread, give energy over time. People's bodies use stored fat for energy when carbohydrates are[75] low. Storing too much fat, however, slows people down.

Proteins help build and repair the body. Fish and beans are good sources of protein.

Vitamins[100] and minerals also have particular jobs. For example, the Vitamin C in oranges keeps teeth strong. The mineral iron in nuts keeps blood healthy.[124]

The foods with the widest stripes on the food pyramid are the ones that are most important in a balanced diet.

# The Food Pyramid

Few foods contain all five nutrients. To get all five nutrients, people must eat different kinds of foods. The food pyramid shows [25] the balance of foods that people need to stay healthy.

The most important foods are shown with the widest stripes in the pyramid, while the [50] least important foods are given the thinnest stripes. Grains have the widest stripe on the pyramid because they are a big part of a balanced [75] diet. Meats are given a thinner stripe on the pyramid because they are a smaller part of a balanced diet.

Fat, which is the thinnest [100] stripe on the pyramid, is needed in only tiny amounts. Because sugar is digested quickly, sweets are not a part of the food pyramid. [124]

# Food and Nutrition

**Nutrition Facts**

Serving Size 8 fl oz (240 mL)
Servings per container about 7

Amount Per Serving

| Calories 110 | Calories from Fat 0 |
|---|---|

**% Daily Value***

| | |
|---|---|
| **Total fat** 0 g | **0%** |
| Saturated Fat 0 g | **0%** |
| **Cholesterol** 0 mg | **0%** |
| **Sodium** 0 mg | **0%** |
| Potassium 450 mg | **13%** |
| **Total Carbohydrate** 26 g | **9%** |
| Sugars 22 g | |
| **Protein** 2 g Not a significant source of protein | |

| | |
|---|---|
| Vitamin C 120% | Calcium 2% |
| Thiamin 10% | Niacin 2% |
| Vitamin B6 4% | Folate 15% |
| Magnesium 6% | |

Not a significant source of dietary fiber, vitamin A and iron

* Percent Daily Values are based on a 2000 calorie diet.

**Nutrition Facts**

Serving Size 1 package
Servings Per Container 1

Amount Per Serving

| Calories 150 | Calories from Fat 90 |
|---|---|

**% Daily Value***

| | |
|---|---|
| **Total fat** 10 g | **15%** |
| Saturated Fat 3 g | **15%** |
| **Cholesterol** 0 mg | **0%** |
| **Sodium** 180 mg | **8%** |
| **Total Carbohydrate** 15 g | **5%** |
| Dietary Fiber 1 g | **4%** |
| Sugars 0 g | |
| **Protein** 2 g | |

| | |
|---|---|
| Vitamin A 0% | Vitamin C 0% |
| Calcium 0% | Iron 0% |

* Percent Daily Values are based on a 2000 calorie diet.

Nutrition labels help you build a balanced diet. What differences do you see between the nutritional values of these foods?

# Nutrition Labels

Labels describe the nutritional value of foods and drinks. Knowing a food's nutritional value can help people build a balanced diet.

An orange[25] has about 70 calories, but it supplies all of the Vitamin C that people need in a day. In addition, oranges are full of complex[50] carbohydrates, so people don't get hungry right away.

A small bag of potato chips has about 150 calories, which are mostly from fat. Potato chips[75] also have sodium, a mineral in salt. Because salty foods make people thirsty, people often drink soda with potato chips. Soda adds calories, sodium, and[100] sugar to a person's diet. Nutrition labels show you that an orange provides more nutrients than a bag of potato chips and a soda.[124]

# Food and Nutrition

The human body uses water in many ways. To stay healthy, people need to replace the water they use.

# Water Supply

In addition to food, people need a constant supply of water. Water's importance goes beyond the minerals and vitamins that are in some[25] waters.

About two-thirds of the human body is made up of water. Water helps a person digest food, use nutrients, and maintain an even[50] body temperature. A person needs a constant supply of water to replace water that is lost through daily body functions.

Part of a person's water[75] supply comes from the water in food, like fruit, and fluids, like juice and milk. Sodas have water, too, but they also have sugar and[100] sodium. Sugar and sodium add to thirst; they don't satisfy it. Water is the best fluid for satisfying thirst and helping body functions.[123]

# Food and Nutrition

People around the world balance their diet by eating many different kinds of foods.

# Bugs for Dinner?

All people need the same nutrients to stay healthy. However, people can get their nutrients from different foods. For example, vegetarians do[25] not eat meat, which has a lot of protein. Instead, vegetarians get protein from foods like beans and nuts.

In many parts of the world,[50] people's diets include insects. While some insects are poisonous to people, more than 1,000 kinds of insects are not poisonous.

Roasted waterbugs are a treat[75] in parts of Asia. In parts of Mexico, crushed stinkbugs are mixed with salsa to add to the salsa's taste. Ground-up ants are used[100] like jam on bread in parts of South America. For many people around the world, insects are a cheap and tasty source of protein.[124]

# Review Food and Nutrition

Write words that will help you remember what you learned.

## Eating Right

_____

_____

_____

_____

## The Food Pyramid

_____

_____

_____

_____

## Nutrition Labels

_____

_____

_____

## Water Supply

_____

_____

_____

## Bugs for Dinner?

_____

_____

_____

_____

## Eating Right

1. What are nutrients?

   Ⓐ kinds of foods that give people energy

   Ⓑ the carbohydrates that are in foods

   Ⓒ kinds of vitamins that people need every day

   Ⓓ the parts of food that keep people healthy

2. What is the difference between simple and complex carbohydrates?

   _____

   _____

   _____

## The Food Pyramid

1. The food pyramid shows _____

   Ⓐ only the foods that have the most nutrients.

   Ⓑ how to eat a balanced diet.

   Ⓒ why grains are an important part of a healthy diet.

   Ⓓ every food that people need to eat every day.

2. Why do you think the most important foods are shown with the widest stripes on the food pyramid?

   _____

   _____

   _____

## Nutrition Labels

1.   What do nutrition labels show?

    Ⓐ how much a food costs

    Ⓑ a food's nutritional value

    Ⓒ how to cook a food

    Ⓓ what a person should eat at each meal

2.   How can nutrition labels help you plan a balanced diet?

_____

_____

_____

## Water Supply

1.   "Water Supply" is MAINLY about _____

    Ⓐ why water is important to people's health.

    Ⓑ why water keeps the body's temperature even.

    Ⓒ why soda doesn't satisfy people's thirst.

    Ⓓ why people need lots of different kinds of water.

2.   Name two reasons people need water.

_____

_____

_____

## Bugs for Dinner?

**1.** Why do people eat insects?

    Ⓐ They are a good source of carbohydrates.

    Ⓑ They are a good source of fat.

    Ⓒ They are a good source of protein.

    Ⓓ They are a good source of fruits and vegetables.

**2.** What are two different ways people get protein into their diet?

_____

_____

_____

## Connect Your Ideas

**1.** How can nutrition labels and the food pyramid help you stay healthy?

_____

_____

_____

**2.** You are sitting down to a meal of chicken, green beans, potato chips, an apple, and a soda. Which parts of the meal are healthful? How could you make the meal more healthful?

_____

_____

_____

# Civil Rights Leaders

Dr. Martin Luther King, Jr., is shown leading a march for civil rights in the United States in 1965.

# Civil Rights

People have certain private, or civil, rights in the United States. Today, people of all races, genders, and religions have civil rights, including[25] the rights to vote in elections and to be treated fairly. The Declaration of Independence, which established the United States as a country, states that[50] "all men are created equal." However, men of some races and women of all races could not vote and were not treated fairly when the[75] Declaration of Independence was written.

Since that time, amendments have been added to the Constitution of the United States. These amendments promise civil rights to[100] people of all races, genders, and religions. Such laws and amendments to the Constitution exist because certain Americans worked hard for civil rights.[123]

Susan B. Anthony worked hard for equal rights.

# Equal Rights

As a teacher in 1850, Susan B. Anthony believed it was wrong that women could not own land or vote. She also believed[25] it was wrong that most African Americans were slaves with no civil rights. She decided to devote her life to gaining equal rights for all[50] men and women.

In 1870, the 15th Amendment gave men who had been slaves the right to vote. Anthony was disappointed that the 15th Amendment[75] did not help women. She took 10,000 names of people who wanted women's rights to the U.S. Senate, but the Senate would not listen to[100] her. Susan B. Anthony died in 1906, disappointed that women could not vote. In 1920, women were finally given the right to vote.[123]

Thurgood Marshall worked to make sure that all children have the right to an equal education.

# Equal Education

In the 1950s, some towns had separate schools for white and black children. Often, white children's schools had better facilities than black children's[25] schools. Because many black children's schools had poor facilities, a lawyer named Thurgood Marshall believed that black children did not have the same rights as[50] white children.

Thurgood Marshall argued for children's rights to an equal education in front of the Supreme Court. Marshall argued that all children should have[75] the same education, at the same time, and in the same place. The Supreme Court agreed. Separate schools for children of different races were not[100] allowed.

In 1967, Thurgood Marshall became the first African American justice on the Supreme Court, where he supported civil rights for all people.[123]

# Civil Rights Leaders

In this picture, President Lyndon Johnson meets with civil rights leaders after signing the Voting Rights Act of 1965.

# Equal Treatment

Even with amendments to the Constitution, some people could not vote in elections and were not treated fairly at work and in public[25] places. President Lyndon B. Johnson, the 36th President of the United States, worked with Congress to pass two acts that made such practices unlawful.

Before[50] the Civil Rights Act of 1964, some businesses and public places refused to serve or hire people because of their race, gender, or religion. This[75] act made these practices unlawful.

Before the Voting Rights Act of 1965, some towns required people to pass a reading test or pay a tax[100] to vote. This act made these practices unlawful. Americans' civil rights are protected by law because of the leadership that President Johnson provided.[123]

Marian Wright Edelman started the Children's Defense Fund to make sure that children were treated fairly.

# Children's Rights

Neither the Declaration of Independence nor the Constitution describes the rights of children. Just 100 years ago, no American states had laws against[25] children working full-time. At that time, children as young as six years old worked long days in factories all year round. In 1938, an[50] act of Congress made it unlawful for businesses to employ children younger than 14, or younger than 16 when school is in session.

Today, Marian[75] Wright Edelman is a leader for children's rights. In 1973, she started the Children's Defense Fund to work for children's safety, health, and fair treatment.[100] Marian Wright Edelman leads the Children's Defense Fund in supporting children's rights, including providing free health care and passing laws that protect all children.[124]

Write words that will help you remember what you learned.

## Civil Rights

_____
_____
_____
_____

## Equal Rights

_____
_____
_____
_____

## Equal Education

_____
_____
_____
_____

## Equal Treatment

_____
_____
_____
_____

## Children's Rights

_____
_____
_____
_____

## Civil Rights

**1.** The main idea of "Civil Rights" is that _____

    Ⓐ the Declaration of Independence gave civil rights to all people.

    Ⓑ people in the United States have the right to vote.

    Ⓒ the United States was begun by civil rights leaders.

    Ⓓ all Americans have civil rights today.

**2.** What are two civil rights that all of the people of the United States have today?

_____

_____

_____

## Equal Rights

**1.** What did the 15th Amendment to the Constitution do?

    Ⓐ It gave all adult men the right to vote.

    Ⓑ It gave men who had been slaves the right to vote.

    Ⓒ It gave all adult women the right to vote.

    Ⓓ It gave men who had been slaves and women the right to vote.

**2.** What are two rights Susan B. Anthony wanted all people to have?

_____

_____

_____

# Review Civil Rights Leaders

## Equal Education

**1.** Another good name for "Equal Education" is _____

Ⓐ "Schools for Every Town."

Ⓑ "The Supreme Court."

Ⓒ "Thurgood Marshall's Fight."

Ⓓ "Changes at the Supreme Court."

**2.** What kind of rights did Thurgood Marshall work for?

_____

_____

_____

## Equal Treatment

**1.** "Equal Treatment" is MAINLY about _____

Ⓐ how towns passed laws for civil rights.

Ⓑ laws that make sure all people are treated fairly in the United States.

Ⓒ how businesses refused to serve or hire some people.

Ⓓ why Lyndon B. Johnson became President of the United States.

**2.** What did the Civil Rights Act of 1964 do?

_____

_____

_____

## Children's Rights

**1.** The Children's Defense Fund works for _____

    Ⓐ people who defend children.

    Ⓑ children who are younger than 14.

    Ⓒ children who want to work.

    Ⓓ fair treatment for children.

**2.** Why is Marian Wright Edelman called a civil rights leader?

_____

_____

_____

## Connect Your Ideas

**1.** Choose two of the people you have read about in this unit. Describe why they are called civil rights leaders.

_____

_____

_____

**2.** What qualities do you think a person needs to have to be called a leader?

_____

_____

_____

# The 50 American States

In this picture, people are writing and talking about the Constitution of the United States.

# American States

More than 200 years ago, representatives of the 13 colonies met to write the Constitution of the United States. While the representatives wanted [25] the country to be "united," they also wanted the states to be important. Small states did not want bigger states to dominate them. None of [50] the 13 colonies wanted the national government to dominate the states in everything. Each colony wanted its people to be heard.

The Constitution of the [75] United States describes the rights of states and citizens. A state can tax its citizens and make laws, as long as the laws don't go [100] against the laws of the Constitution. When compared with other countries, the United States is unique in the power of its state governments. [123]

# The 50 American States

Shown here is the capitol building of the state of California. This is where California's state legislature meets.

# State Governments

The 50 American states are different in many ways, including size. The state with the most people is California, with over 37 million[25] people. The state with the fewest number of people is Wyoming, with fewer than 0.5 million people.

No matter what size they are, all 50[50] states have a governor, a state legislature, and courts. State legislatures make laws and tax people to pay for services, such as schools, roads, and[75] state parks.

While all states have a governor and a legislature, each state decides how often its legislature meets. California has a legislature that meets[100] nine months every year. Wyoming has a legislature that meets 40 days in one year and 20 days in the next year.[122]

# The 50 American States

These California students are working together on a school project.

# Learning and Playing in States

State governments are responsible for the place where children spend a lot of their time—schools. State governments decide how[25] long a school year should be. In most states, children must go to school for 180 days a year. However, children in North Dakota go[50] to school for 173 days, while children in Texas go to school for at least 180 days. States make other decisions about schools, such as[75] which tests students will take at the end of the year.

All states have also set aside land for parks that people can enjoy. Driving[100] through Rhode Island, America's smallest state, takes only about one hour. In this small area, Rhode Island has more than 20 state parks, beaches, and forests.[126]

KANSAS

The Western Meadowlark and the Common Sunflower are symbols of the state of Kansas. The sunflower appears on the state flag.

# State Symbols

Each state has its own history and identity. States use symbols, such as nicknames, flags, birds, and flowers, to show their unique identities.[25]

A state's nickname often tells something unique about the state. Delaware is nicknamed "the First State" because Delaware was the first state to agree to[50] the U.S. Constitution. Kansas is nicknamed "the Sunflower State" because sunflowers grow on the Kansas plains in great numbers.

The cardinal is the most common[75] state bird. Seven of the 50 American states use the cardinal as their symbol.

Each state also has a unique flag. Often, a symbol, such[100] as a flower or a bird, appears on the state flag. For example, the sunflower is on the state flag of Kansas.[122]

# The 50 American States

Local governments use the taxes people pay to provide services, such as people to fight fires.

# Local Governments

What would life be like if trash covered the sidewalks or if police officers and firefighters were not there to respond to problems?[25] States are divided into counties that include several towns or cities. Counties and towns have local governments that provide services, such as trash pick-up,[50] and people to help us, such as police officers and firefighters.

Local governments are usually responsible for public libraries and for many of the parks[75] where soccer and other games are played. In some places, local governments are responsible for hospitals, too.

Often, national and state governments help local governments.[100] For example, when a town needs a new hospital or library, national and state governments may give money to build them.[121]

Write words that will help you remember what you learned.

## American States

_____

_____

_____

_____

## State Governments

_____

_____

_____

_____

## Learning and Playing in States

_____

_____

_____

_____

## State Symbols

_____

_____

_____

_____

## Local Governments

_____

_____

_____

_____

## American States

**1.** "American States" is MAINLY about _____

&#9400; how the 13 colonies were formed.

&#9401; how the Constitution of the United States was written.

&#9402; why the states of the United States have power.

&#9403; why the United States has national laws.

**2.** Why did the Constitution give so much power to the states?

_____

_____

_____

## State Governments

**1.** Which of the following do all states have?

&#9400; a governor and a legislature

&#9401; a state legislature that meets every year

&#9402; the same amount of state taxes

&#9403; courts that make laws for the state

**2.** What are two things state legislatures do?

_____

_____

_____

# Review The 50 American States

## Learning and Playing in States

1.  Another good name for "Learning and Playing in States" is _____

    Ⓐ "What State Legislatures Do."

    Ⓑ "State Schools and State Parks."

    Ⓒ "What Children Need to Know."

    Ⓓ "The Laws State Legislatures Make."

2.  What are two things that states are responsible for?

    _____

    _____

    _____

## State Symbols

1.  The main idea of "State Symbols" is that _____

    Ⓐ many states chose the cardinal as their state bird.

    Ⓑ states use symbols to show their identities.

    Ⓒ every state has a state flag.

    Ⓓ nicknames tell something unique about a state.

2.  Why might a state want to have a symbol?

    _____

    _____

    _____

## Local Governments

**1.** What are some things local governments do?

    Ⓐ provide services such as trash pick-up and libraries

    Ⓑ divide states into counties and towns

    Ⓒ give money to build armies and hospitals

    Ⓓ run the national and state governments

**2.** How do national and state governments help local governments?

_____

_____

_____

## Connect Your Ideas

**1.** Suppose there was another passage in this unit. Would you expect it to be about how laws are made or how different birds live? Why?

_____

_____

_____

**2.** What are two ways your life would be different if there were no governments?

_____

_____

_____

Container ships carry products around the world, linking people through trade.

# The World Community

The United States is separated from all countries, except Mexico and Canada, by oceans or long distances. However, no matter how long[25] the distances to other countries, Americans depend on people all around the world. Everyone breathes the same air. Americans depend on other countries to keep[50] Earth's environment healthy. Other countries also depend on the United States to keep Earth's environment healthy.

Americans count on other countries to supply materials for[75] products and to buy products that Americans make. Other countries also count on the United States to supply materials and buy products they make.

As[100] a member of the world community, the United States helps other countries in many ways. It is helped by other countries in many ways, too.[125]

# The United States and the World Community

The flags in front of the United Nations headquarters in New York City are from the countries of member nations.

# The United Nations

The United States and most of the world's countries belong to the United Nations. Each member nation sends representatives to the United[25] Nations headquarters in New York City. At the United Nations headquarters, representatives work to solve problems between countries that could lead to wars.

The United[50] Nations has other aims, too, such as improving the health of children around the world. In many countries, children can't turn on a tap when[75] they are thirsty to get clean water. Instead, they go to rivers or wells for water. Often, this water isn't clean, and it may carry[100] diseases. The United Nations works to get clean water to children everywhere on Earth. Making water safe to drink helps to prevent diseases.[123]

This Peace Corps volunteer is teaching people about health care in South America.

# The Peace Corps

When John F. Kennedy became President of the United States in 1961, he asked Americans to use their skills to aid those[25] in need. President Kennedy began the Peace Corps so that Americans could help people around the world.

People who volunteer for the Peace Corps work[50] to improve schools, health care, and farms in other countries. Because of the work of Peace Corps volunteers, many countries now have better schools, health[75] care, and farms.

Only adults can be Peace Corps volunteers. However, students in schools like Corcoran High School in New York can help Peace Corps[100] projects. In 20 years, Corcoran High School students have made almost $100,000 from selling cards and T-shirts to aid Peace Corps projects in Africa.[124]

# The United States and the World Community

In this picture, athletes from around the world are holding up a giant Olympic flag.

# The Olympic Games

Every four years, more than 10,000 athletes from about 200 countries compete in the summer Olympic Games. Olympic athletes share the goal[25] of performing at the highest level in their sports. As they get to know one another, the athletes learn that people from many countries share[50] the same dreams and face the same challenges.

Each Olympics is held in a different city around the world. Visitors from many countries come to[75] see the Olympics. About a billion people watch the Olympics on television. Visitors and television viewers also learn that people around the world share dreams[100] and challenges. During the Olympic Games, people from many countries watch sports together and often learn that they share many other interests.[122]

# The United States and the World Community

The Mir space station helped scientists from the United States, Russia, and other countries learn about space.

# The International Space Station

The United States is leading a partnership of scientists from 16 countries to keep people living on a space station that [25] orbits Earth. Since November 2, 2000, people have been living at the International Space Station and studying space. A team of scientists travels to the [50] station in a space shuttle and usually stays for five months. Then another team takes its place.

The international partnership began with the Russian space [75] station Mir, which orbited Earth for 15 years. Americans, Russians, and others lived and worked on Mir.

Information from Mir helped scientists in the partnership [100] build the International Space Station. At the space station, scientists perform experiments on how things work in space. Scientists also study Earth from space. [124]

Write words that will help you remember what you learned.

## The World Community

_____
_____
_____
_____

## The United Nations

_____
_____
_____
_____

## The Peace Corps

_____
_____
_____
_____

## The Olympic Games

_____
_____
_____
_____

## The International Space Station

_____
_____
_____
_____

## The World Community

**1.** Another good name for "The World Community" is _____

- Ⓐ "Keeping the Environment Healthy."
- Ⓑ "Buying the World's Products."
- Ⓒ "Countries Around the World."
- Ⓓ "All Countries Are Connected."

**2.** What are two ways that people around the world count on one another?

_____

_____

_____

## The United Nations

**1.** The main idea of "The United Nations" is that the United Nations _____

- Ⓐ works to clean the world's water.
- Ⓑ helps children prevent diseases.
- Ⓒ works to solve problems around the world.
- Ⓓ protects the environment in its member nations.

**2.** Name two things the United Nations does.

_____

_____

_____

## The Peace Corps

1.  The Peace Corps works to _____
    Ⓐ improve life for people around the world.
    Ⓑ help people in the United States make money.
    Ⓒ improve life for people in the United States.
    Ⓓ help people in other countries become volunteers.

2.  In what three ways do Peace Corps volunteers help people?

    _____

    _____

    _____

## The Olympic Games

1.  "The Olympic Games" is MAINLY about _____
    Ⓐ how people can become Olympic athletes.
    Ⓑ how a city is chosen for the Olympic Games.
    Ⓒ the kinds of sports athletes play in the Olympics.
    Ⓓ how the Olympic Games bring the world together.

2.  What are two things you think people could learn by performing in or watching the Olympics?

    _____

    _____

    _____

## The International Space Station

**1.** Which of the following is a fact about the International Space Station?

    Ⓐ It stays in space for five months at a time.

    Ⓑ It is run by a partnership of countries.

    Ⓒ It is run by Russia.

    Ⓓ It has been orbiting the Sun for 15 years.

**2.** What are two things scientists do at the International Space Station?

_____

_____

_____

## Connect Your Ideas

**1.** Suppose there was another passage in this unit. Would you expect it to be about U.S. history or international law? Why?

_____

_____

_____

**2.** Why do you think it is important for people in the United States to care about what is happening around the world?

_____

_____

_____

# Reading Log • Level E • Book 1

| | I Read This | New Words I Learned | New Facts I Learned | What Else I Want to Learn About This Subject |
|---|---|---|---|---|
| **Marine Animals Without Backbones** | | | | |
| Marine Invertebrates | | | | |
| Stingers | | | | |
| Mollusks | | | | |
| Outer Skeletons | | | | |
| Sea Stars | | | | |
| **Plants and People** | | | | |
| Plants and Life on Earth | | | | |
| The Biggest and the Best | | | | |
| Pluots and Apriums | | | | |
| Special Ways to Grow Plants | | | | |
| What's Next for People and Plants? | | | | |
| **Food and Nutrition** | | | | |
| Eating Right | | | | |
| The Food Pyramid | | | | |
| Nutrition Labels | | | | |
| Water Supply | | | | |
| Bugs for Dinner? | | | | |

| | I Read This | New Words I Learned | New Facts I Learned | What Else I Want to Learn About This Subject |
|---|---|---|---|---|
| **Civil Rights Leaders** | | | | |
| Civil Rights | | | | |
| Equal Rights | | | | |
| Equal Education | | | | |
| Equal Treatment | | | | |
| Children's Rights | | | | |
| **The 50 American States** | | | | |
| American States | | | | |
| State Governments | | | | |
| Learning and Playing in States | | | | |
| State Symbols | | | | |
| Local Governments | | | | |
| **The United States and the World Community** | | | | |
| The World Community | | | | |
| The United Nations | | | | |
| The Peace Corps | | | | |
| The Olympic Games | | | | |
| The International Space Station | | | | |

# Self-Check Graph

Record your reading rate her

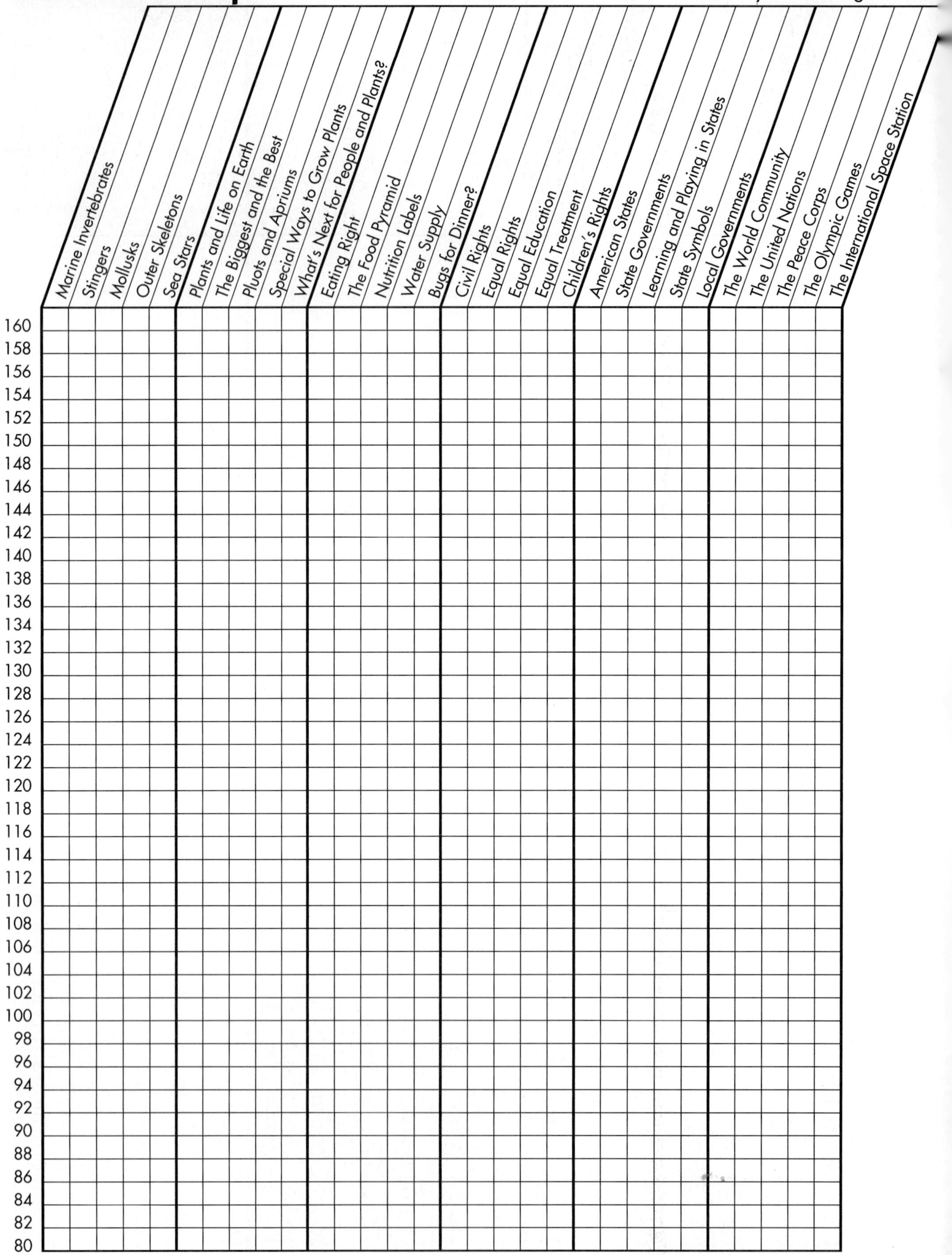

Marine Invertebrates
Stingers
Mollusks
Outer Skeletons
Sea Stars
Plants and Life on Earth
The Biggest and the Best
Pluots and Apriums
Special Ways to Grow Plants
What's Next for People and Plants?
Eating Right
The Food Pyramid
Nutrition Labels
Water Supply
Bugs for Dinner?
Civil Rights
Equal Rights
Equal Education
Equal Treatment
Children's Rights
American States
State Governments
Learning and Playing in States
State Symbols
Local Governments
The World Community
The United Nations
The Peace Corps
The Olympic Games
The International Space Station
160
158
156
154
152
150
148
146
144
142
140
138
136
134
132
130
128
126
124
122
120
118
116
114
112
110
108
106
104
102
100
98
96
94
92
90
88
86
84
82
80